CURLY LAMBEAU

Other Badger Biographies

CURLY LAMBEAU
BUILDING THE GREEN BAY PACKERS

STUART STOTTS

WISCONSIN HISTORICAL SOCIETY PRESS

Published by the Wisconsin Historical Society Press
Publishers since 1855

Publication of this book was made possible, in part, by gifts from the following donors:
Mrs. Harvey E. Vick of Milwaukee, Wisconsin
Green Bay Packers

wisconsin history.org

Photographs identified with PH, WHi, or WHS are from the Society's collections; address inquiries about such photos to the Visual Materials Archivist at the above address.

Printed in the United States of America
Designed by Jill Bremigan

13 12 11 10 09   2 3 4 5 6

Library of Congress Cataloging-in-Publication Data

Stotts, Stuart, 1957-
  Curly Lambeau : building the Green Bay Packers / Stuart Stotts.
     p. cm. – (Badger biographies)
  Includes bibliographical references and index.
  ISBN 978-0-87020-389-3 (pbk.)
  1. Lambeau, Curly, 1898-1965. 2. Green Bay Packers (Football team)–History. 3. Football coaches–United States–Biography. 4. Football–United States–History. I. Title.
  GV939.L25S86 2007
  796.332'640977561–dc22
                                        2007026334

Front and back cover photos: courtesy of the Neville Public Museum of Brown County

Contents

1

Salt Sack Football

Lambeau Field is one of the great landmarks in Green Bay. Loyal fans know it's the home of the Green Bay Packers. But where did the name Lambeau come from? The man most responsible for making the Packers a professional football team and for keeping the team in the small city of Green Bay was Curly Lambeau.

Modern Packer fans often wear foam "cheesehead" hats.

When Curly Lambeau was a boy in the early 1900s, he and his friends played with a small burlap salt sack stuffed with sand, leaves, and pebbles. They couldn't afford a ball. They kicked the filled sack back and forth and tried to run past each other with it. Adding gravel to the sack made it easier to throw accurately. In the fall they gathered in the vacant lots and parks of Green Bay to choose teams and engage in rough-and-tumble games of what was then still a fairly new and unknown sport—football.

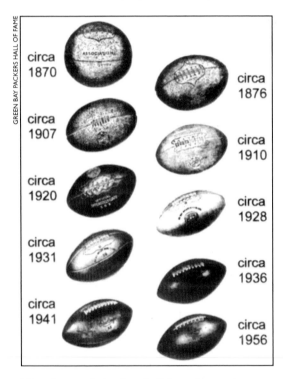

GREEN BAY PACKERS HALL OF FAME

circa 1870

circa 1876

circa 1907

circa 1910

circa 1920

circa 1928

circa 1931

circa 1936

circa 1941

circa 1956

The shape of the football has changed over time.

Of course, the "ball" was made from a sack. And its size and shape didn't resemble a modern American football either. The boys' sack-ball was more like a modern soccer ball in size, though not as rounded. This made it difficult to throw very far.

circa: about

In Curly Lambeau's boyhood, there were informal town teams in communities around the country, but there were no professional leagues. Football was mostly a running game. The most common plays were **handoffs** and **dropkicks**. It was unusual for teams to pass more than 2 or 3 times in a game. Teams gained yards by blocking and running as they pounded through the defensive line of the other team. This heavy body contact gave rise to the phrase "3 yards and a cloud of dust" to describe the old-fashioned style of playing.

Fred Hulbert and Town Teams

A man named Fred Hulbert first organized community football in Green Bay in 1895. For the next 25 years, town teams and neighborhood teams competed. Team members changed every year as players came and went. The schedules were casual. Games were often canceled or scheduled at the last minute. Many communities all over Wisconsin had such "town teams" that would challenge each other to games.

handoff: a play in which one player gives the ball to another   **dropkick:** a play in which a player drops the ball and kicks it right after it hits the ground; never used in football anymore

That was the state of football when Earl Louis Lambeau was born on April 9, 1898, to Mary and Marcel Lambeau. He was the oldest of 4 children. Even as a baby, he had thick, wavy hair, which led to his lifelong nickname of "Curly." Marcel's parents had come from Belgium, and Mary's family was originally from southern France. Both of Curly's parents' families had come to Wisconsin in the 1870s. They were part of a **thriving** European immigrant community in Green Bay at the time.

Green Bay was very different when Curly was born in 1898 than it is today. This shot of the city dates from around 1900.

thriving: doing well

Green Bay's Immigrant Population in the 1900s

In the 1900s, Green Bay was a center for 3 industries: papermaking, cheese making, and large meatpacking. Many who lived and worked there were fairly recent immigrants from Germany, Poland, Ireland, and Belgium, just like Curly's family. People were, by and large, **cautious** (**kaw** shuhss) and **law-abiding** (**law** uh **bye** ding) citizens.

Curly's family first lived at 615 North Irwin Street in a simple red brick house. Then the Lambeaus moved to a little 2-story house at 1205 Cherry Street, where Curly shared a bedroom with his brothers, Raymond and Oliver. His sister, Beatrice, had her own room. Marcel Lambeau was in the construction business. Although the family was not poor, they did have to be careful with their money.

The Lambeau family lived in this simple red brick house on Irwin Street before moving to Cherry Street.

cautious: trying hard to avoid mistakes or danger   **law-abiding:** obeying the laws of a government

Curly was a large, solid, strong boy. Even then, he oozed confidence, especially when it came to athletics. He played football from an early age. He watched every game he could, wherever the game was played: at a high school, a city park, or a vacant lot.

In eighth grade, Curly joined his first organized team at Whitney Grade School. He led the team to victory over the East High freshman team. But Curly also broke his ankle

during the season. It was the only serious injury he ever received in his entire career as a player.

In eighth grade, Curly joined his first organized team at Whitney Grade School.

The next year at East High School, Curly was a starter on the football team, and he received **letters** all 4 years for playing. He was a great runner. His strength, speed, and size meant he could run right past or right over would-be tacklers. He kicked

letter: a fabric letter that can be sewn on a sweater to show that a player who plays on a high school team is important to the team

well and could accurately drop-kick a **field goal** from 40 yards. However, Curly stood out from other players of the time. Not only did he have great ability, but he also loved to pass the ball. That was rare in football games of the time. The following year, the *Green Bay Press-Gazette* wrote about him, "Lambeau is a **sophomore** (**sof** mor)…. He weighs 175 pounds and is an expert in the sending department of the forward pass game."

Curly's senior year at East High gave him new opportunities to prove himself. Curly was elected captain, and he called the plays. The coach from the previous year hadn't returned. The new coach assigned to the team didn't know anything about football. After a few practices, he told Curly to take over, even though Curly was just a student! With the help of 3 local fans, Curly ran the team that season.

In the early days of football, only players on the field were allowed to call plays. Coaches were forbidden to tell the players what to do during the game.

field goal: a goal made by kicking the ball through the arms of the upright stands at the goal line
sophomore: a student in the second year of high school or college

East High School's biggest rival was Green Bay West High School. By Curly's junior year, West had beaten East 7 years in a row. Curly had a great season as a senior. He scored most of East's touchdowns, and he did most of the team's **punting** (**puhnt** ing), dropkicking, and passing. He badly wanted a win over West to cap his high school career. East came into the game undefeated. On Thanksgiving Day, 1916, Curly led his team to a 7-6 victory over West. The local paper, the *Green Bay Press-Gazette*, reported that Lambeau "dimmed the playing of the other men on the [2] teams...[with] great ground gaining, heavy booting and hectic defense....[He was] in every play." He gained 165 of East's total yards. In fact, he gained more yards by himself than all the yards gained by the whole West team.

It's important to remember that at that time, passing was still a new and different way of playing football. West fans were surprised and angry about East's **strategy** (**strat** uh jee). They shouted, "Why don't you run the ball?"

punting: kicking the ball to give it to the other team   **strategy:** the plan a team uses to play the game

All through high school Curly was a great all-around athlete. As captain of the track team, he competed in **shot put, discus, and broad jump**. He won honors at the Northeast Wisconsin Regional track meet during his senior year. People knew and recognized him all over town. Although Curly had a growing **reputation** as an athlete in many sports, football remained his first love.

EAST HIGH SCHOOL YEARBOOK, 1917

Curly in his track uniform in his high school yearbook

UW SPORTS INFORMATION

As captain of the high school track team, Curly competed in shot put, discus, and broad jump. The left and center images show Olympic athlete Arlie Mucks throwing shot put and discus. A broad jumper is on the right.

shot put, discus, and broad jump: track competitions that involve throwing and jumping   **reputation:** a person's worth or character as judged by other people

TOM MURPHY

Curly with his girlfriend,
Marguerite Van Kessel

Curly had a girlfriend, a young woman from East High School named Marguerite Van Kessel. Marguerite was a year younger than Curly. She was an excellent student and a fine piano player. She and Curly spent lots of time together when Curly wasn't involved in sports.

10

2

To Notre Dame and Back Again

After graduating from high school in 1917, Curly worked in the summer for his father's construction business. In the fall, he went to the University of Wisconsin–Madison. Curly really went to the university just to play football. He dropped out after only a month because the Madison freshman football team program was canceled, and freshmen couldn't play on the varsity team. Curly returned to Green Bay and worked for his father.

Later that fall, Curly played football with his childhood friend, Nate Abrams. Nate worked in his family's cattle business. Like Curly, he loved playing football. Nate and Curly played on an All-Star Green Bay team against a Marinette team in a game to raise money for the Red Cross. Curly ran for 2 touchdowns and threw a scoring pass to Nate to lead Green Bay to a 27–0 victory.

After the season, Curly did construction work through the winter and spring. The work made him stronger. He also spent a lot of time with his high school girlfriend, Marguerite.

Nate Abrams

Friends in Green Bay urged Curly to return to college. In particular, they wanted him to attend Notre Dame (no **tur** dame). Although now a university, at the time Notre Dame was a small Catholic college in South Bend, Indiana. It didn't have the reputation in sports that it has now, but over the years it had usually fielded a winning team.

In the fall of 1918, Curly played one game with a town team called the Skidoos, and then he headed off to enroll at Notre Dame. He used the money he had made working for his father to pay his college expenses. Classes and other activities besides football did not interest him much. Curly arrived at Notre Dame just as the legendary Knute Rockne (**noot rock** nee) became head coach.

Knute Rockne: Notre Dame's Famous Coach

NOTRE DAME SPORTS INFORMATION DEPARTMENT

Knute Rockne played football at Notre Dame as a student, but he was never a great player. Later, he became assistant coach. In 1918 he was named head coach of the team. Even as an assistant coach, he had already begun to change the way football was played at Notre Dame.

At the time, most football games consisted of running with the ball and smashing hard into the defensive line, hoping for a gain of 2 or 3 yards.

The legendary Knute Rockne, Curly's coach at Notre Dame

Brute strength meant everything for winning.

Rockne's system depended on speed, brains, and complicated plays. He coached the players to work around big players rather than trying to go through them. He also encouraged them to throw forward passes. This strategy could help the team gain big yardage.

Knute Rockne was also known for his speeches, or pep talks, to his players. He had the best winning record in history of any football coach. His teams won 88 percent of their games. In fact, his lifetime record was 105 victories, 12 losses, and 5 ties. Knute Rockne was the most famous coach of his time.

brute: using a lot of strength instead of skill or intelligence

13

While Curly was at Notre Dame, so many young men were helping the United States fight World War I that the football season of 1918 was shortened to only 6 games. Curly made Notre Dame's team as a **halfback** and **fullback**. He was bigger and stronger than most of the other players, and he scored the first touchdown in the season's first game against Case Tech. This is the way the Notre Dame **roster** described Curly: "**flamboyant** (flam **boy** uhnt) one-year player for Rockne in shortened season. Excellent blocker and good short-yardage runner. In 1918 started as fullback....Scored first touchdown of season in win over Case. Scored 2 touchdowns in **slaughter** (**slaw** tur) of Wabash. Rushed for effective short yards in win over Purdue and in tie with Nebraska."

Curly liked playing football at Notre Dame. He took pride in being an athlete. He liked wearing the blue and gold team sweater. He liked sitting at a special table in the dining hall, and he liked being recognized around campus. But Curly was lonely. He wrote letters home every day, mostly to Marguerite. In one letter he said, "Dear Marguerite, words cannot explain

halfback: one of the backs stationed near the far left or right side   **fullback:** an offensive back used primarily for line plunges and blocking   **roster:** a list of people   **flamboyant:** colorful and flashy   **slaughter:** win by a wide margin

14

NOTRE DAME SPORTS INFORMATION DEPARTMENT

Curly Lambeau was a halfback and fullback on Notre Dame's 1918 team.

how bad I want to be with you tonight. I never thought I would miss you so." Curly was far from home, and although he was a good player, he wasn't the best on the team. After being so well known in Green Bay, he missed being the center of attention.

At the end of the semester, Curly went home to Green Bay for Christmas with a bad case of **tonsillitis** (ton suh **ly** tiss), which required surgery. The doctor couldn't operate for 6 weeks, until the infection improved. Curly couldn't return to Notre Dame after winter break. By the time his health had improved, Curly had fallen too far behind in his studies to catch up. He decided not to go back to Notre Dame at all. He stayed in Green Bay, hungry for his next football opportunity.

tonsillitis: a throat infection

3

Town Team on the Move

While Curly was away at college, his friend Nate Abrams had organized an all-city football team called the Green Bay Whales. George Whitney Calhoun, a reporter for the *Green Bay Press-Gazette* newspaper, became the team manager. The Whales played against teams from nearby towns. That season they had outscored their **opponents** (uh **poh** nuhnts) by a total of 216 to 17, even without Curly's help.

After Curly returned to Green Bay, Nate introduced him to Frank Peck. Frank ran a meat company called the Indian Packing

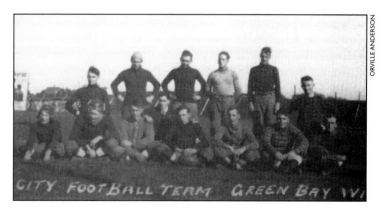

Green Bay Whales

opponent: someone who is against you in a fight, contest, debate, or election

17

Company. Nate's own cattle business had worked with Frank Peck's company, and Nate thought Frank and Curly would like each other.

Later that winter, Curly met Frank Peck on the street one day. They decided to have lunch together. Frank already knew that Curly was an extraordinary athlete. During lunch, Curly's intelligence and personality impressed Frank. He offered Curly a job as a shipping clerk at the plant. Curly's starting pay was $250 a month, which was a very high salary at that time.

Curly worked at the packing plant through the spring and summer. Marguerite's sister, Ruth, also worked there. Curly walked to their house in the mornings to get a ride. He often got there early and tossed a pebble against Marguerite's window, so she would look out. He talked with her before he went to work.

During the summer, Curly met with George Calhoun, the reporter who had managed the Whales football team the previous year. They talked about starting a football team in the fall and decided to hold a meeting to see who might be interested in playing.

Curly asked his boss, Frank Peck, if the Indian Packing Company would be willing to sponsor a football team. In those days, companies often sponsored sports teams as a way of advertising. Frank was swayed by Curly's ideas, and he agreed to give the team $500 for uniforms. Frank also agreed to let them practice on an empty field near the plant. In exchange, the team uniforms would carry the Indian Packing Company's name.

In mid-August, 2 meetings were held to start the team. On August 11, 1919, Curly and George Calhoun met with interested players. Many of them had played the previous year on the Whales team. Three days later, on August 14, the team was formally organized. Calhoun served as manager and Curly as captain.

Although this was a new beginning for the team members, their name was a little unclear. At first they were known as the Big Bay Blues, but that name didn't stick. On August 15, the day after the meeting, the *Green Bay Press-Gazette* ran an article with the headline "Indian Packing Company **Squad (skwahd)** Meets; First Game Sunday, September 14." Later in the article, the team was referred to as "the Packers." That first game **signaled** the beginning of what became the Green Bay Packers.

George Calhoun played a key role in the success of the team. George was a classic old-time sportswriter. He chewed on cigars and spoke gruffly as

PRESS-GAZETTE, FRIDAY EVENING, AUG

GREEN BAY PRESS GAZETTE, AUGUST 15, 1919

CURLY LAMBEAU CHOSEN CAPTAIN OF FOOTBALLERS

Indian Packing Corporation Squad Meets; First Game on Sunday, Sept. 14.

"Curly" Lambeau, former East High and Notre Dame football star, was elected captain of the Indian Packing Corporation's team at the meeting last night of the city footballers in The Press-Gazette. G. W. Calhoun will again manage the eleven this season.

Close to 25 pigskin chasers attended the conference last evening and there was a good deal of enthusiasm displayed among the candidates. It was the unanimous opinion that, if Green Bay doesn't get away with state honors this year she never will.

Practice will start September 3, the Wednesday following Labor day, and

from then on it will be held three times weekly, Mondays, Wednesdays and Fridays.

Providing a suitable opponent can be secured, the Packers will open the season on Sunday, Sept. 14, at Hagemeister park. Up to date the only game closed on the schedule is with Marinette here on Oct. 26. Many other arguments are now pending and it is expected that at least three more arguments will be booked during the coming week.

Shooting.

Close of Grand American handicap tournament at Chicago.

Tennis.

National doubles championship tournament at Boston.

Brother Moose.

Howdy Pap! Don't miss the big meeting, Friday night. Class initiation followed by corn roast and smoker. Officers and members should attend. Chas. J. Williams, Sec'y.

Girl for house work, 709 School Place.

In 1919, Curly was chosen as the coach of the Indian Packing Company football team.

he spouted opinions about everything. In order to get fans to attend, he bragged about the Packers in his newspaper columns. He insulted their opposing teams and built up **expectations** (ex pek **tay** shuns) for every game. Without George's enthusiasm and ability to get an audience for the

squad: another name for a team   **signaled:** sent a message or warning   **expectation:** an idea or belief about what should happen

20

Sportswriter George Calhoun helped manage the Green Bay Whales and later helped publicize the Packers.

games, the Packers might have remained just another town team.

Mid-August 1919 was important for Curly in other ways. On August 16, he and Marguerite were married in Green Bay. They spent their honeymoon traveling to towns around the state so that Curly could arrange games for the Packers. Although this honeymoon wasn't a very romantic start to a marriage, Marguerite loved Curly. She supported him because she saw how driven he was to organize his new team.

4

Packers' First Season

When Curly Lambeau and his Packers team began to play, professional football was just beginning to move from being a local to a regional sport. Wisconsin had many "town" teams in cities such as Beloit, Green Bay, and Racine. Even more common were the neighborhood teams that often played one other.

NEVILLE PUBLIC MUSEUM OF BROWN COUNTY

The Packers' first official season in 1919 was incredibly successful. The team won 10 games, all by hugely **lopsided** scores such as 87–0

Curly posed as if he were receiving a snap from the center.

lopsided: unbalanced, with one side heavier, larger, or higher than the other

and 76-6, with a total point score of 565-12! Although they lost their last game to Beloit, it was a close game. Many Green Bay fans thought that the **referees** in that game were unfair to the Packers. That first season, Curly did most of the running and the passing. He also played defense.

The Beloit Fairies were the first team to defeat the Packers.

Curly had always liked to pass the football. In one of the early games against Ishpeming, Michigan, he learned he had to pass if he wanted to win. The opposing team was filled with big, strong players. On the first 3 plays, 3 Packers were knocked out of the game by injuries. Curly was afraid he would run out of players, because only 20 men traveled with his team. By passing the ball, the players made less physical

referee: someone who supervises a sports game and makes sure the players follow the rules

23

contact with their opponents. This decreased the number of their injuries. Green Bay won 53-0. From that day forward, the Packers became known as a passing team.

The Packers home games were played at Hagemeister (**hawg uh mey stuhr**) Park in Green Bay. There were no seats. Fans stood behind the roped-off area or drove close and sat in their cars to watch the game. There were no tickets or admission fees. George Calhoun,

A game at Hagemeister Field

Boys would climb trees to see the games being played at Hagemeister Field.

24

the manager, walked through the audience and collected donations. On a good day he might get $200. He had to take money out to pay for expenses and injuries. Then Calhoun divided up the remaining money to pay the team. At the end of the season, each player had earned $17.

The following year, Curly's father built wooden **bleachers** at Hagemeister Park. Instead of collecting donations, the Packers began to sell tickets. They sold 1,200 for the first game. The fans were not disappointed. That season, the Packers won 9, lost 1, and tied 1. At the end of the season they had outscored their opponents 227-24.

From 1919 to 1921, Curly also coached the East High School football team. There, his record was 14 wins, 4 losses, and 3 ties. In 1920 he was particularly delighted to beat West, East's big rival. He wrote, "We beat West...with passing. I remember the West fans didn't like it. They said, 'Run the ball, that's not football.'"

bleacher: a raised seat or bench arranged in rows

The Popularity of High School Football

Curly left East after 1921 so he could focus on the Packers. Still, over the next few years, more fans watched the East-West game than would typically attend a Packers game. In 1925, 5,300 fans watched the Packers play the Bears at City Stadium, but more than 7,000 watched the 2 Green Bay high school teams play in the same spot. In that decade, high school football was just more popular.

In December 1920, Curly and Marguerite had their only child, a son. They named him Donald. Although Curly must have been a proud father, he was never close to Donald. Sadly, Curly's focus on his work left little time for being a father. His first love was football, and he gave it all of his attention.

When the season was over, George Calhoun heard about a new professional football league being formed in Ohio. It was called the American Professional Football Association. League members were planning a meeting in August of 1921.

Curly badly wanted the Packers to play in the new league—
he wanted the Packers to face tougher competition, and he
wanted to be more famous.

That same year, the Acme Packing Company bought the
Indian Packing Company. Curly had a new boss, John Clair.
Curly convinced him to attend the new league's meeting to
get a **franchise** (**fran** chize) for Green Bay. John Clair liked the
idea of wider **publicity** (puh **bliss** uh tee), and the company
also hoped to make some money from the team. Between the
company's support and Curly's **ambition** (am **bish** uhn), the
Packers were ready for the big leagues.

franchise: a license to operate a professional sports team   **publicity:** information about a person or an event
that is given out to get the public's attention or approval   **ambition:** a strong wish to be successful

5

Present at the Birth of the NFL

John Clair sent his brother Emmett to Chicago in August 1921 to buy a franchise in the new American Professional Football Association. The franchise cost $50. The Association had 21 teams spread across the nation. George Calhoun announced in the *Green Bay Press-Gazette* that Green Bay had been given a spot in a professional football league. Enthusiasm for the Packers grew rapidly. Citizens helped to build 1,000

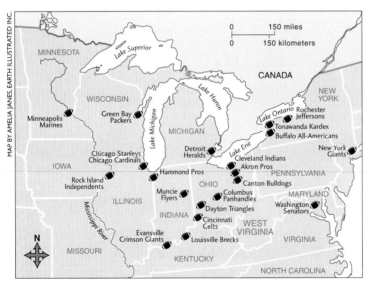

American Professional Football Association teams in 1921

more seats, and the nearby Elks Club agreed to let the players use their showers. Now the team would not have to change into their uniforms at home.

Curly in #20 jersey

Although the Packers officially belonged to the Acme Packing Company, Curly Lambeau was the heart of the team. He was the star player, the **strategist** (**strat** uh jist), and the captain. Curly was not the coach, but he was really the one in charge. He was also a powerful salesman for the team. Curly spoke at civic events to promote ticket sales. His reputation as a player made him a star in his hometown, and he enjoyed being a **celebrity** (suh **leb** rih tee).

Curly hired a player named Howard "Cub" Buck, who had played one game with the Packers the previous season. He was the first player to whom Curly **guaranteed** a salary, and he received $75 per game. The other players' salaries depended on how much the team took in at a game. Buck was a huge

strategist: someone who plans out how the team will play   **celebrity:** a famous person   **guaranteed:** promised that something would happen

lineman. His size and strength ensured that the Packers could easily defeat their opponents. Curly was determined to do everything he could to make his team a winner.

Going into that season, the Packers' uniforms had Acme Packers in big letters across the front. In the 1920s, players didn't have big pads to protect

Lineman Howard "Cub" Buck was the first player to whom Curly guaranteed a salary. Buck earned $75 per game.

1921 Packers team

themselves. Their helmets were made of leather and could be folded up and put into a player's pocket! Some players rolled up magazines and used them for shin guards. The rules weren't as strict. Referees weren't always fair, and player injuries were common.

Early Professional Teams

At one time, Milwaukee, Kenosha, and Racine all had football teams that were part of the early National Football League. Only Green Bay's team survived in the league.

The Packers won their first 4 games against local teams. In more **competitive** (kuhm **pet** uh tiv) league play, however, the Packers weren't so successful. They ended with a season record of 3 wins, 2 losses, and one tie. Out of the 21 teams in the league, the Packers finished in seventh place that first season. The 1921 season marked a big change for the Packers in other ways. Although they still played against local and regional teams, the Packers were no longer just a town team. Now they were members of a national league. They played

competitive: more difficult

31

against teams from other parts of the country. Curly had set
his sights on being part of something bigger, and the Packers
had begun to make that change.

Curly was a good salesman for the team, but it was George
Calhoun who really pumped people up. He made sure that
the *Green Bay Press-Gazette* often had articles about the
team. He also encouraged people to attend games that were

played out of town. The
Packers even had their own
band called "the Lumberjack
Band." Its musicians dressed
in plaid shirts, red caps, and
rubber boots. They played at
all home games and began to
attend away games as well.

The Lumberjack Band

For all its success, the Packers' first season as a professional
team ended badly. They had paid college players to play,
which was against the rules. Many other teams broke this
rule, but the Packers got caught and were kicked out of
the league. Emmett Clair had to go to a league meeting in

December to return the franchise. Green Bay was suddenly without a professional football team.

At the urging of some Green Bay businessmen, Curly applied to reclaim the franchise. The league had just changed its name to the National Football League (NFL) when Curly attended a league meeting in June. After some discussion, the league granted him the rights to the team for $1,000. Curly borrowed the money from his friend Don Murphy. At 24 years old, Curly was now the owner of the Green Bay Packers.

The 1922 season ended with a record of 4 wins, 3 losses, and one tie, but the Packers had lost money. The Packers had guaranteed to pay 2 teams more than $2,000 dollars each for coming to play in Green Bay. Bad weather meant low attendance at both games. Suddenly the Packers were several thousand dollars in **debt** (**det**). Although Nate Abrams loaned the Packers money, it wasn't enough.

Curly met with several key Packers backers who had put up money for the team. They had to figure out how to save the Packers from **financial** (fuh **nan** shul) ruin. In order to

debt: an amount of money or something else that you owe   **financial:** having to do with money

33

raise the money to pay for another season, they decided to sell **shares** in the team. Anyone who bought a share owned a piece of the Packers. One share cost $5, and anyone who bought 5 shares got a guaranteed box seat at all home games. George Calhoun and the Packers backers let people and businesses know that because the Packers were an important part of the community, they deserved help. The Packers backers held meetings and ran advertisements. Slowly they raised the money they needed to keep the team alive. This group of men ran the Packers for many years and made it possible for the team to survive.

By selling shares in the team, Curly gave up his ownership. The Green Bay Packers, **Incorporated** (in **kor** puh rate ed), became a **nonprofit corporation**. The team donated any **profits** (**prof** it) to the American Legion. The citizens of Green Bay and Wisconsin *still* own the team! No one makes any profit from it. The Green Bay Packers, Incorporated, is unique. No other professional sports team in the United States has a similar form of organization.

share: one of many equal parts into which a business is divided   **incorporated:** made part of a legal business corporation   **nonprofit corporation:** a business whose main purpose is something other than making money   **profit:** amount of money left after all of the costs of running a business have been subtracted from the money earned

Curly Lambeau played a major role in **fund-raising (fuhnd rayz ing)**. When the fund-raising was finished, he turned his attention to building a strong team. He knew

This stock certificate from 1923 shows that Ernest Stiller owned 5 shares of stock in the Green Bay Packers. Wisconsin citizens still own the football team today. It is the only professional sports team in the United States that is a publicly owned nonprofit corporation.

that the only way to make enough money to keep supporting the Packers was to have a team that people wanted to watch. Curly and the Packers needed to win, and they needed to win *big*.

fund-raising: collecting money for a specific cause

6

Bringing Home Championships

Curly Lambeau had an intense drive to win. He was a star player, but now he devoted most of his energy to his role as coach. First, he searched throughout the country for the best players. Then he worked to convince them to play for Green Bay. By 1923, Curly was the only Packer left who had started on the original town team 3 years earlier. Curly was so eager to win that he quickly cut players and replaced them with more talented ones. Curly also kept an eye on expenses, and he'd cut a player if he thought that the player was asking for too much money.

Curly wasn't easy to work for, either. He pushed his team very hard in practice. He frequently lost his temper with players when he felt upset with the team's performance. When the team lost a game, Curly wasn't shy about pointing his finger at someone whom he thought was responsible for the loss. However difficult Curly was for his players, his efforts and strategies paid off. The Packers improved. Between 1923 and 1928, they won 43 games, lost 20, and tied 8. This record made them one of the best teams in the NFL. They made money, too, although not very much. In the 1923 season, for example, the team made $147.74. That was certainly better than losing money, as the Packers had in previous seasons.

In the 1920s, baseball was much more popular than professional football in the United States. Huge crowds filled baseball stadiums, and players such as Babe Ruth captured fans' imaginations. When it came to football, college games were far more popular than professional games. College games might draw 70,000 fans, while 8,000 would be a huge crowd for a professional football game.

GREEN BAY PACKERS HALL OF FAME

Curly often lost his temper on the sidelines.

Professional football also had a bad reputation. People bet heavily on games, and many suspected that the games were **fixed**. In the mid-1920s, however, professional

College football games were more popular than professional ones, as this well-attended 1929 University of Wisconsin game shows.

football's popularity began to grow. When the Chicago Bears hired a well-known college football star, Red Grange, the sport began to receive national attention.

Every NFL team benefited from having Red Grange in the league, and attendance at Packers games grew. In 1925, the Packers moved into City Stadium next to East High School. Curly's father's company had built this stadium specifically for the team. The stadium increased its seating every year, but it still had only the most basic features. While there were some box seats, there were no restrooms. Men relieved themselves

fixed: games in which gamblers illegally pay players to lose on purpose

38

under the stands, while women just had to wait until they got home. Games usually lasted only 2 hours, so this wasn't as difficult as it would be today. The seats were made of 2-by-12-foot planks, with lots of space between them. So many fans dropped purses and hats and other possessions during the game that the Packers had security guards under the stands to retrieve the fallen items and take them to the lost and found.

In the 1920s, Curly's teams played well, and the fans kept coming to games. The Packers impressed national newspapers with their abilities. They beat teams from larger cities such

WHI IMAGE ID 3673

Aerial view of City Stadium

as the New York Giants. The intense **rivalry** (**rye** vuhl ree) with the Chicago Bears was in full swing. More than 2,000 Green Bay citizens traveled to Chicago to watch the Packers beat

the Bears in 1928. The Packers were a well-respected team, but they had not yet proved themselves champions.

rivalry: an ongoing competition between 2 teams

Green Bay Packers vs. Chicago Bears

ASSOCIATED PRESS

The Chicago Bears–Green Bay Packers rivalry is the oldest, and probably the strongest, in professional football. That rivalry goes all the way back to the beginning of the league. In 1921, Bears coach George Halas was responsible for having the Packers thrown out of the league. He was the one who reported that the team included college players.

George Halas and Curly didn't like each other, and their feelings affected their teams. For example, one year George Halas sent Curly a telegram saying, "Please take it easy

George Halas was the coach of the Chicago Bears. Halas and Curly were strong rivals.

on my Bears, as we have many injuries." Curly knew it wasn't true. Each coach would spy on the other before games. On game day, they wouldn't speak to each other. Curly said, "Shake hands? That would have been a lie. If I lost, I wanted to punch Halas in the nose. If he lost, Halas wanted to punch me." Over the years, Curly and Halas developed respect for each other. Still, the rivalry between the Green Bay Packers and the Chicago Bears remains strong, if far friendlier, today.

Curly played regularly through 1927. He put in a few appearances on the field in 1928 and 1929. By the end of 1929, his playing days were over. But his glory days as a coach were just beginning.

Curly recruited players from around the country. They became part of a championship **dynasty** (**dye** nuh stee). Some star players became the center of the first great Green Bay Packers teams. Curly chose players well. Clarke Hinkle, a powerful runner and tackler, said, "Curly could see things in a ballplayer that other coaches couldn't." His ability to choose players helped the team to gain its good reputation.

From 1929 through 1931, the Green Bay Packers were champions in the NFL. No team had ever won 3 championships in a row. The Packers beat teams from the United States' biggest cities, such as New York and Chicago. They were undefeated in 1929. Over these 3 seasons they won 34 games, lost 5, and tied 2 others. Curly Lambeau's team was known all over America. Curly himself became the best-known figure in football.

dynasty: in football, a team that wins consistently over several seasons

Curly was featured on magazine covers and in sports articles. Although no longer a player, he was in great shape. He was always confident and self-assured. He dressed well. He loved to talk with reporters, and the Packers received great press coverage all over the country. Curly was on top of the game, and everyone knew it. City Stadium now had 10,000 seats. For a popular game, such as one against the Chicago Bears, 13,000 people could squeeze in. Curly Lambeau was always interesting to watch at a game. He strutted up and down the sidelines, shouting, cursing, and gesturing. He was an **imposing** (im **poze** ing) figure, confident and **animated** (**an** i may tid). He enjoyed the attention that came from winning.

Curly Lambeau's players respected and feared him. Many of them didn't like him. One of his most famous players from that time, Cal Hubbard, said, "They won't be able to find 6 men to bury the so and so.... He drove us hard, but he got the job done." Remember that Curly was quick to fine players for mistakes or for breaking the rules.

imposing: impressive and grand   **animated:** lively

42

Clarke Hinkle said, "Curly Lambeau was the founder, creator, and coach. But I never really liked him...[nor] respected him, either, but he was paying me and I gave 1,000 percent every time I played...."

There's a story that in 1929, the last season Curly played, the players were angry at Curly for yelling at them so much. During one play when he carried the ball, no one blocked for him, and the opposing team piled on him. It may have hurt Curly, but it didn't change his style.

Curly enjoyed designing plays, but it wasn't his strongest feature as a coach. Several of the Packers thought that they had to change the plays he created in order to be successful on the field. Hubbard recalled, "Sometimes Curly would design a play and we knew it just wouldn't work the way he had designed it...one of the **veterans** (**vet** ur uhn) would go right up to the blackboard and change it around." Still, Curly cared a lot about designing plays. His wife said that sometimes he would wake up with ideas, and she would find

---

veteran: a player who has been a member of a team for many seasons

43

the pillowcase covered with Xs and Os, where he had diagrammed plans that had come to him at night.

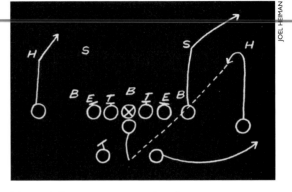
Xs and Os in a passing play diagram

Whatever his play making abilities may have been, Curly was an **innovator** (in uh **vay** tur) in early football's style of play. He was the first coach to take his players through daily practices, pushing them to excellence.

Diagramming Plays

Coaches had to come up with ideas for plays, in order to show each player what he should do. This is known as "designing a play." Coaches usually drew plays on paper or chalkboards, **diagramming** (**dye** uh gram ing) each player's assignment.

Curly diagramming plays at the blackboard

diagramming: drawing to explain a play **innovator:** someone who takes a new and original approach

44

In 1938, he became the first coach to fly his team to distant games, instead of taking trains or buses. He was one of the first coaches to move a player from the backfield up to the line, to make another man available to go out for passes. And, of course, his **emphasis** (**em** fuh sis) on the forward pass kept him on top of the game for many years.

The Packers were one of the first teams to travel to games by airplane.

Curly always wanted his players to present a good public image. Clarke Hinkle remembered, "Whenever we went out on the road, he'd make us wear suits, coats, ties." At the time, people were not aware of the health risks of cigarette smoking, but many thought the habit was sinful. Clarke Hinkle recalled, "He wouldn't let us smoke in public because people might think less of us."

Curly had to manage his players carefully. Some of them got into trouble with the law or didn't want to follow his rules. He was quick to get rid of players who didn't obey him.

emphasis: importance given to something

But if a player was very good in the game, Curly did what he needed to keep him ready to play. That didn't stop Curly from being demanding. He shouted and threatened, and his team fairly consistently did what he asked. Most players described him as a great **motivator** (**moh** tuh vay tur). Clarke Hinkle remembered, "He believed in pep talks, and he would inspire us. Before we went out on the field, he'd have us jumping through the windows...[with excitement]."

Curly sold life insurance on the side. He liked to wear good clothing. He was a good-looking man, and he enjoyed all the attention. When he was out in public, he carried his cash in a roll of bills. He loved to peel off a 10 or 20 dollar bill to pay for something, just so that everyone could see how much money he had.

The enthusiasm of Green Bay fans grew as the team became more successful. Long before television, when the Packers played away from Green Bay in the 1920s, people would gather at Turner Hall to watch a play-by-play re-creation of the game on the "Gridograph," also called the

motivator: someone who can make others feel enthusiastic and able to accomplish necessary tasks

"Playograph." The Gridograph showed the names of the players from each team on opposite sides of a large board. The action from the game would be **telegraphed** (**tel** uh graft) to Green Bay, and an announcer would describe what was happening. Men behind the board moved a small white wooden football to whichever player had possession. This showed people what was happening in a crude sort of way.

Fans often traveled with the Packers to out-of-town games, and other towns noticed the enthusiasm of the team supporters. When the team won the championship in 1929, the streets of Green Bay were filled with waving admirers.

NEVILLE PUBLIC MUSEUM OF BROWN COUNTY

Fans watch the Packers from behind a fence at Hagemeister Park.

telegraphed: sent a message in Morse code over a wire

They whistled, yelled, and honked car horns. Traffic was at a standstill. The players were given a hero's welcome. Each received a new watch and a check for $220—a lot of money at the time. This kind of **reception** (ri **sep** shuhn) showed just how much Green Bay loved Curly Lambeau and his Packers.

Newspaper headline announcing 1929 championship

reception: response

7

Sliding Downhill

As football became more popular throughout the United States, the Green Bay Packers were the most successful team. Millions of people recognized Curly Lambeau. Even though the Packers didn't win a championship in 1932, they were asked to come and play **exhibition** (ek suh **bish** uhn) **games** in Hawaii after the season ended.

When the Packers returned from the games, Curly went to Hollywood to talk with people in the movie industry. He was interested in helping filmmakers to make a movie about football. Although the actual movie never happened, Curly was affected by his time in Hollywood. Curly liked being famous, he liked being around famous people, and he liked the **glamour** (**glam** ur) associated with Hollywood.

exhibition game: a game against a nonconference team **glamour:** fashion, charm, or appeal

When he returned to Green Bay, more than football was on his mind. This change was not good for Curly or the Packers. His Hollywood adventures marked a negative turning point in his life, at home and as a coach.

The glamorous life took a toll on Curly's marriage. His wife Marguerite divorced him in 1933. Curly had been spending too much time in Hollywood with movie stars, and she was tired of long absences. Two years later, Curly married a young Hollywood model named Susan Johnson. Marrying Susan was another step away from his hometown life in Green Bay. The marriage lasted only 5 years.

As the 1930s went on, the best teams in the league—the Chicago Bears, the New York Giants, and the Green Bay Packers—were also the teams that had been around the

Curly with players

longest. Curly was working hard to put together another
championship team. The NFL had started a college **draft**, and
teams had to take turns choosing players. It was harder for
Curly to get good players, and his skill at selecting players
wasn't as sharp as it had been in the previous decade.

The 1930s was the time of the **Great Depression**, when
many people lost their jobs. Few people had extra money to
spend on sports events. Despite their success, the Packers

draft: a process of professional teams taking turns choosing new players   **Great Depression:** the decade of the
1930s when many people in the United States had no jobs and were very poor

51

were in financial trouble once more. They owed more than $20,000. Once again, a group of supporters stepped in and began to raise money from the Green Bay business community. Despite some changes in the business, people still owned stock in the team.

Don Hutson holding 10 footballs, one for each of his receiving records

Curly did not want to pay his players as much as they demanded, especially when times were tough. The Packers were out of debt by 1937, but Curly remained tight with wages. He was known to bargain hard to get players to play for as little as possible.

In 1935, Curly signed Don Hutson to the Packers. Hutson became one of the greatest pass receivers of all time. The Packers quarterback, Arnie Herber, could throw the ball a long way, which fit perfectly with Hutson's speed. They became a powerful offensive combination, and they helped the Packers become national champions again the following year.

The Packers couldn't seem to find a winning streak. In 1936, the Packers won the championship, but in 1938, they lost the championship game to the Giants. In 1939, the Packers beat the Giants, 27-0, in Milwaukee to win their fifth championship in 11 years. But in 1941, World War II began, and every team lost many of its players to military service. The Packers were affected more than most. They lost 34 veterans and draft choices that year.

In 1940, Curly was named second vice president in the Packers organization and was put on the board of directors. Although it was unusual for a coach to be part of the governing group of a team, the stockholders were grateful to Curly for being so successful. Other NFL owners wanted the Packers to move to a larger city where they could make more money from larger attendance, but Curly fought to keep the Packers in Green Bay. He understood, however, that the number of Green Bay fans had to keep growing to keep ticket sales high. He acted as a salesman for the team. He spoke at public functions to advertise the Packers whenever he could.

From 1940 to 1943, the Packers had strong winning records, but the Chicago Bears proved to be stronger. They always finished ahead of the Packers. In 1944, the Packers again won the championship, but in 1945, the Packers finished third in their division. It was the first time they hadn't ended up in first or second place in more than 10 years.

Curly had been running the same offensive patterns for more than 20 years, but times had changed. When the Bears won the championship in 1940, it was partly because they started to use a new formation, called the T formation. The T formation is still used in modern football. In the T formation, the quarterback stands right behind the center to get the ball. Soon other teams began to adopt it as well. But Curly

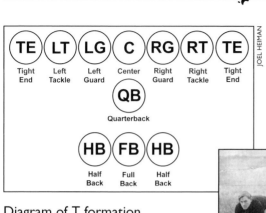

Diagram of T formation

Players in T formation

stuck with the game he knew and understood, where the
quarterback stood farther in the backfield. It wasn't until 1947
that he adopted the T formation and began to catch up with
modern ideas. But by then, the Packers had fallen behind other
teams and weren't winning as often.

Although Curly was successful for a long time, in the end,
his failure to change was one reason the Packers could not
keep their winning streak.

8

Losing Games, Losing Faith

In 1945, World War II ended, and many athletes returned to play football. The Packers, however, were still missing key players.

That same year, Curly married once again, this time to Grace Garland, a wealthy California woman. She knew many famous people. Grace and Curly traveled around the country together during the off-season. They often attended fancy parties.

In 1945, Curly married Grace Garland. Curly is pictured here with Grace and her daughter.

Curly enjoyed the glamorous life, but the people of Green Bay thought that Curly had "gone Hollywood" and was losing touch with his roots. When the Packers didn't play well, they blamed Curly. They thought that his team and his hometown were no longer very important to him.

When Curly started to spend more time in California, many people said he'd lost his connection with Green Bay or "gone Hollywood."

The NFL was expanding. More cities wanted teams. The All-America Football Conference (AAC), a brand-new league, competed with the NFL for fans and for players. The NFL wanted to move the Packers to a larger city where the team might make more money. But the team's directors refused. The owners of the team—the citizens of Green Bay and Wisconsin—would never have allowed the NFL to move the Packers.

Curly had a hard time replacing the players he had lost to the war and to retirement. When Don Hutson retired, Curly no longer had a good pass receiver. The Packers had to change their game. Now they were forced to run the ball and rely on the defense. The Packers actually had an excellent running game that year, but it wasn't enough. The season ended with 6 wins and 5 losses, the worst record since 1934. A headline in the *Green Bay Press-Gazette* read: "It's Hard To Imagine The Packers Without Passing, But It's True." Curly needed someone who could pass the ball well.

Curly was still involved in the management of the team as its vice president. In 1947, he fired longtime friend George Calhoun, who had been in charge of publicity for the Packers. Curly resented the way Calhoun criticized him about the team's poor performance. Calhoun had also criticized Curly's personal life.

This was the same George Calhoun who had helped Curly put the team together back in 1919 and who had been a tireless supporter. He had raised money at games in the early days. He had written articles and built up the Packers in every way he could. Fans liked Calhoun, and they thought that Curly had treated him badly.

Worst of all, Calhoun learned that he had been fired by reading about it in the newspaper! Curly didn't have the courage to tell him face-to-face. Curly replaced Calhoun with a sportswriter friend from Chicago. Calhoun remained on the board of the team, and he became even more strongly opposed to Curly's actions in team affairs.

That same year, Curly made several bad coaching decisions in close games, which led to another poor record. People in Green Bay wondered if Curly still had the ability to bring Green Bay a winning season. Curly hadn't had a great record in 3 years. That was a long time for the Green Bay football fans, who were used to winning. Between a bad Packers season and Curly's mistreatment of George Calhoun, fans lost faith in Curly's magic.

Things didn't improve the following season. Injuries hurt the team, and for the first time ever, the Packers lost 4 games in a row. In Green Bay, fans complained even louder. At the

GREEN BAY PACKERS HALL OF FAME

Coach Lambeau

end of the losing season, Curly talked about the reasons things had gone poorly. He didn't take much blame for it himself, however. He was happy to take the credit when the Packers were winning, but he spread the blame around when they lost. This kind of attitude didn't help to rebuild support for his coaching and decision making.

In 1949, Curly announced that he was giving most of the coaching duties to his 3 assistant coaches. He would dedicate himself to finding new players to bring back a winning team. Green Bay fans were shocked by the announcement. For the first time in nearly 30 years, Curly wasn't the coach in charge. Some thought that Curly knew the players weren't very good and that he didn't want to take responsibility for a losing team. Although he shuffled and traded and cut players, the team still ended up 2-10, the worst record ever. Attendance dropped off at games, too. Once again, the Packers were in financial trouble.

As the season ended, the NFL and the AAC agreed to **merge (murj)**. Some of the AAC teams would be added to the NFL, creating one league. The merger started new rumors that the Packers might move away from Green Bay.

Players and fans in Green Bay were unhappy with Curly Lambeau. There were meetings and discussions. People took sides. Rumors flew. Finally, on January 31, 1950, Curly Lambeau **resigned** from the Packers.

merge: join together   **resigned:** gave up a job, a position, or an office voluntarily

61

Curly's fall from favor was complicated. He had made some bad decisions. He also had made some enemies, such as George Calhoun and the team's doctor, W. W. Kelly, whom Curly had also fired. People accused Curly of spending too much money from his **expense account** (ek **spenss** uh **kount**). People thought he no longer cared about the city and the team.

Curly had wanted to be in charge, but others who managed the Packers organization had put limits on how much he could do alone. Curly's time in Hollywood took his attention away from the game, and he couldn't attract the players he needed to rebuild the team after World War II. Then there were the years in the 1940s when Curly had failed to adapt his style of play and use the T formation.

All of these poor decisions made Packers fans lose faith in Curly and in his ability to build and keep winning teams. That loss of faith turned the fans against him. Perhaps people had expected too much of one man's abilities. Yet Curly had, in many ways, made himself larger than life. Now he could no longer live up to the image he had worked hard to create.

expense account: money given to coaches to cover costs such as food, transportation, and hotel rooms

Still, in Green Bay, many fans couldn't believe he would really leave. Some worried about the future of the Packers, because there was the constant threat that the team would move to a larger city. But other fans believed that it was time for a change. They were hungry for a winner again, and they wanted someone who would focus entirely on Green Bay.

9

Leaving and Returning

State Historical Society Madison, Wis. Complimentary

GREEN BAY PRESS-GAZETTE

28 PAGES

FREE PRESS ESTABLISHED IN MAY 1914
GAZETTE ESTABLISHED IN FEBRUARY 1861

GREEN BAY, WIS., WEDNESDAY EVENING, FEBRUARY 1, 1950

ASSOCIATED PRESS
UNITED PRESS

PRICE 5c

Lambeau To Coach Chicago Cardinals

Argue Court Order Against Coal Miners

Labor Practices Unfair, Charge By Government

No Reply Given Yet To Truman Proposal For 70-Day Truce

WASHINGTON — (P) — The government today argued to a federal court that current coal strikes and slow downs are unfair labor practices. It asked the court to order John L. Lewis and his miners to stop these tactics.

The case is that brought by Robert Denham, National Labor Relations board counsel.

President Truman has said that Denham acted on his own, but had advised the White house of his

Experts Think U.S. Can Make Hydrogen Bomb Within Year

Nation Remains Ahead of Russia in Arms Race, Belief; Truman Decision Approved

From Press Dispatches

With the United States going ahead full blast on development of a hydrogen super-bomb in an obvious effort to win the atomic arms race with Russia, U.S. experts said that the nation will produce and test its first hydrogen weapon within the year.

Reaction ranged from general agreement with President Truman's decision among members of congress, through emphasis particularly in the United Nations and aimed at the need for international atom controls, to Communist criticism.

President Truman, in his announcement Tuesday giving the green light to the H-bomb project, said development would proceed until an effective means of world atomic control—including Russia—is assured.

Tighten Guards At Atom Plants

Extra Precautions for Overhead Patrol Taken By Defense Department

Leader of Packers For 31 Years Quits

Will Also Become Vice-President Of Club, Submits Resignation Here

Earl L. (Curly) Lambeau, coach of the Green Bay Packers for 31 years, today was named coach of the Chicago Cardinals of the National American football league.

Lambeau signed a two-year contract. Ray C. Bennigsen, Cardinal president, said he would also serve as a vice president of the club and would be in complete charge of player personnel. His appointment is effective immediately.

No salary was announced for the 30-year veteran of pro football ways, but there was speculation that it probably called for a big part of money \$20,000 a year and possibly provides for a bonus depending on the gridiron success of the team and attendance.

Mrs. Violet Bidwill, owner of the club, said she was "extremely happy over the acquisition of Lambeau as her coach." She was in Miami Beach, Fla., vacationing.

Mailed Resignation

Packers Ready To Carry on, Fischer Says

Will Start Search For Coach at Once

The Green Bay Packers corporation will begin immediately the selection of a head football coach to replace E. L. (Curly)

Members of the joint congressional atomic committee talk with Atomic Energy Commissioner Sumner T. Pike (right) at a meeting Tuesday afternoon to discuss ways and

Curly left the Packers to coach the Chicago Cardinals in 1950.

Immediately after leaving the Packers, Curly was offered a new job as head coach and vice president of the Chicago Cardinals. The Cardinals had never had very good teams. They hoped that the legendary Curly Lambeau would turn things around. But Curly seemed tired of coaching. He didn't insist on good practices, and he let his assistants handle much of the work. By the end of the season, the Cardinals had won 5 and lost 7, and Cardinals fans were already calling to get rid of Curly. The following year, the Cardinals ended with 3 wins and 9 losses, but Curly resigned before the end of the season. Once again, he refused to take any responsibility. He blamed coaches and players for the poor showing, even though he had coached without much effort or interest. Curly's

Curly with Chicago Cardinals coaching staff members

reputation in the NFL was sinking.

Curly wanted to get back into football, but his problems continued. The Washington Redskins hired Curly to be their coach the next year. Like the Cardinals, Washington's team had few good players. To make matters worse, the Redskins' owner had hired and fired 6 head coaches in the previous 14 years! The owner was hard to get along with. Curly's Redskins had 2 poor seasons. Many of the players didn't like playing for him. Once again, Curly couldn't seem to find a solid winning strategy. So, it's not surprising that Curly lost his job with the Redskins at the beginning of his third season. He had a serious disagreement with the owner. For the first time in his life, Curly was fired as coach.

Other areas of his life were also disappointing. Not only was he without a football team, but his third marriage ended in another divorce. Curly spent the winter of 1953 at his ranch in California, and then he headed back to Green Bay. During the summer, he was asked to coach the College All-Stars in their game against the previous year's NFL champions, the Cleveland Browns. Curly had a great victory when his team upset the NFL champs 30–27. He coached the College All-Stars for 2 more years, but they lost both games to the NFL teams.

By 1958, the Packers remained a losing team. Three different coaches had failed to bring home a winner. The Packers were looking for someone to lead them, and Curly's name came up once again. Although he wouldn't say so publicly, Curly wanted another try at the job. However, Packers management didn't want Curly back. In January of 1959, the Packers hired a new coach. His name was Vince Lombardi.

Vince Lombardi

Vince Lombardi is the most famous NFL coach of all time. His success with the Packers in the 1960s led to a lifetime record of 105 wins, 35 losses, and 6 ties. The trophy for the winner of the Super Bowl is known as the Lombardi Trophy, in his honor.

GREEN BAY PACKERS HALL OF FAME

Curly with Vince Lombardi

Curly spent from spring to late fall at his cottage in Door County, and he spent the winters in California. That way he could golf and fish year-round. While in California, he liked to go out to clubs and dance the Twist, the most popular dance of the decade. People said that he became kinder and less

arrogant (**air** ruh guhnt). He enjoyed the success of the Packers under Lombardi, and he became just another enthusiastic fan. Art Daley, a Green Bay sportswriter, remembers how Curly would sit in the press box on game day, filled with positive energy for the Packers, always certain that they would win.

Singer Chubby Checker popularized the Twist, one of Curly's favorite dances.

In 1961, Curly had a TV show in Green Bay called *Ask Curly Lambeau.* He fielded questions and gave his opinions about the Packers. The Packers were very successful at the time under Vince Lombardi. Yet all did not go smoothly between Lombardi and Curly. Lombardi disapproved of Curly's fancy lifestyle, and he also thought that his own contributions mattered more to the Packers and their present fans. Was Green

arrogant: too proud

Bay big enough for 2 football legends at the same time? Lombardi didn't think so.

In 1962, Curly was **inducted** (in **dukt** ed) into the Wisconsin Athletic Hall of Fame. In 1963, he was in the first group to join the Professional Football Hall of Fame. Three of his former players, Don Hutson, Cal Hubbard, and Johnny Blood, were inducted at the same time.

GREEN BAY PACKERS HALL OF FAME

Curly was inducted into the Professional Football Hall of Fame in 1963.

inducted: to be added to an honored group

Curly continued to enjoy a quiet life, splitting his time between Wisconsin and California. On June 1, 1965, Curly was mowing the lawn at a friend's house in Sturgeon Bay. He stopped to show a neighbor how to dance the Twist when he had a heart attack and died suddenly. He was only 67 years old.

The following August, the Green Bay City Council renamed City Stadium Lambeau Field as a tribute to Curly Lambeau. His statue stands in front of the stadium. It reminds all who enter of the **humble (huhm** buhl) origins of one of the greatest NFL teams.

The Green Bay Packers are now an essential part of Wisconsin's image and history. Yet without Curly Lambeau, there would be no Green Bay Packers.

Aerial view of Lambeau Field

His ambition and passion to succeed created a unique sports team and made it into a winner for many years. But when that same ambition and passion went beyond football, they became part of his downfall. His strengths became his weaknesses.

humble: modest and not proud

Perhaps Curly Lambeau believed too much in himself. His pride in the Packers and in his own part in creating them may have made him too proud to listen to the advice of others. That same pride may have made him too stubborn to change his strategies when they no longer worked. Curly also failed to keep the faith of his players. And when he stopped winning, the public stopped supporting him.

Curly *did* return to Wisconsin. He was still a legend, but he also became a fan. In the end, Curly was welcomed home again with honor by Green Bay, a city best known around the world as the home of the Green Bay Packers.

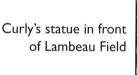

Curly's statue in front of Lambeau Field

SHIRLEY SCRIVER

Appendix

Curly's Time Line

1898 — Curly is born in Green Bay, Wisconsin, on April 9.

1917 — Curly graduates from East High School in Green Bay.

Curly attends the University of Wisconsin–Madison for one month.

1918 — Curly attends Notre Dame in South Bend, Indiana, for one semester.

1919 — Curly meets with George Calhoun, and their discussions lead to a new town team sponsored by the Indian Packing Company.

Curly and Marguerite Van Kessel are married.

1921 — The Packers join the American Professional Football Association (later named the National Football League or NFL).

1929
1930 — Curly wins 3 NFL championships in a row.
1931

1933 — Curly and Marguerite Van Kessel are divorced.

1935 — Curly and Susan Johnson are married.

1940 — Curly and Susan Johnson are divorced.

1936
1939 — Curly leads Packers to NFL championships.
1944

1945 — Curly and Grace Garland are married.

1950 — Curly resigns as coach of the Green Bay Packers on January 31. He is hired by the Chicago Cardinals.

1952 — Curly resigns from the Chicago Cardinals. He is hired by the Washington Redskins.

1954 — Curly is fired by the Washington Redskins.

Curly and Grace Garland are divorced.

1963 — Curly is inducted into the Professional Football Hall of Fame.

1965 — Curly Lambeau dies in Sturgeon Bay, Wisconsin, on June 1.

City Stadium is renamed Lambeau Field in August.

Appendix

The History of Football

To understand Curly Lambeau and the rise of the Green Bay Packers in the world of early professional football, it may be helpful to know something about the sport's early history.

Football is actually a fancy version of "keep-away." One team has something, and the other one wants to get it. Somewhere, centuries ago, a version of keep-away began to be played by kicking a ball and trying to score a goal. This game became what North Americans call soccer and what the rest of the world calls football.

In 1823, at the Rugby School in England, a student named William Webb Ellis picked up a ball during a soccer game and ran with it toward a goal. Although this was against the rules, some of the players and fans liked the idea, and a new game began. In the 1860s, formal rules were adopted for soccer/football and another game known as rugby. From that time, soccer was known as a kicking game, and rugby was a running game.

In the United States, the 2 sports were played side by side in colleges around the country. Slowly, rugby changed and became more like our modern football. By the late 1800s, this game was more popular than soccer. Football teams popped up in colleges and towns around the country. The rules were different from place to place, but the basic idea of running with the ball toward another team's goal was the same.

In 1876, a group of coaches met to attempt to write down rules for American football. Walter Camp, a player and coach at Yale University, began to standardize the game by convincing other teams to agree to the following rules:

MANUSCRIPTS & ARCHIVES, YALE UNIVERSITY. IMAGE #25

- One side keeps the ball until that side loses it by **fumble (fuhm** buhl), by **interception** (in tur **sept** shuhn), or by not gaining enough yardage.

- The line of **scrimmage (skrim** ij) is the spot on the field where the next play begins.

- Play begins by tossing the ball back from the line of scrimmage.

Walter Camp helped standardize football by writing the game's first rules.

- Seven players line up on the line of scrimmage.

- The quarterback, halfbacks, and fullback are behind the line of scrimmage.

- A team surrenders possession of the ball if the team doesn't gain 5 yards in 3 tries, or "downs."

- There are 11 players on a team.

All of these rules and many other rules made Walter Camp the "father of modern football."

Even with these rules, many football players received serious injuries. Some players even died playing. In the "flying wedge," a running wedge of linemen would lock arms or even hold handles that had been attached to their teammates' jerseys. Sometimes teammates would drag ball-carrying players forward. In 1905, 18 players were killed, and

fumble: dropping the ball   **interception:** in football, stealing another team's pass   **scrimmage:** in football, the rough contact that occurs as soon as the ball is picked up off the ground and snapped to another player

football was banned by a number of colleges. President Theodore Roosevelt said that football must be made safer, or he would try to outlaw it!

In 1908, 33 football players were killed. In 1910, dangerous plays like the flying wedge were finally outlawed, and the number of deaths and injuries gradually declined. To help reduce injuries, coaches agreed to the addition of a neutral zone between the scrimmage lines that players could not cross until a play began. Legalizing the forward pass in 1906 also reduced injuries.

In the early years, football players often wore their hair long. They felt that extra padding on their heads would protect them in the rough games of the time. By 1910, football players began to wear helmets and no longer wore their hair long. They also began to wear padding under their clothing to cushion their falls and tackles.

Although college football was popular, professional football was slow to catch on. In 1892 guard William (Pudge) Heffelfinger was paid $500 to play, a huge amount at the time. He was the first known pro football player. The first game played with all paid players was in 1895.

By the early 1900s, contracts between players and teams were common. Clubs often paid college players to join their team. A player might play for his college team one day and for a town team the next. Players also moved from team to team based on who paid more. There was no player draft. The more successful a team was, the better it could pay, and the more good players wanted to play for that team. Curly Lambeau knew this, and built good teams, so that he could attract the best players to the Packers.

Glossary

ambition (am **bish** uhn): a strong wish to be successful

animated (**an** i may tid): lively

arrogant (**air** ruh guhnt): too proud

bleacher: a raised seat or bench arranged in rows

brute: using a lot of strength instead of skill or intelligence

cautious (**kaw** shuhss): trying hard to avoid mistakes or danger

celebrity (suh **leb** rih tee): a famous person

circa: about

competitive (kuhm **pet** uh tiv): more difficult

debt (**det**): an amount of money or something else that you owe

diagramming (**dye** uh gram ming): drawing to explain a play

draft: a process of professional teams taking turns choosing new players

dropkick: a play in which a player drops the ball and kicks it right after it hits the ground; never used in football anymore

dynasty (**dye** nuh stee): in football, a team that wins consistently over several seasons

emphasis (**em** fuh sis): importance given to something

exhibition (ek suh **bish** uhn) **game**: a game against a nonconference team

expectation (ex pek **tay** shun): an idea or belief about what should happen

expense account (ek **spenss** uh kount): money given to coaches to cover costs such as food, transportation, and hotel rooms

field goal: a goal made by kicking the ball through the arms of the upright stands at the goal line

financial (fuh **nan** shul): having to do with money

fixed: games in which gamblers illegally pay players to lose on purpose

flamboyant (flam **boy** uhnt): colorful and flashy

franchise (**fran** chize): a license to operate a professional sports team

fullback: an offensive back used primarily for line plunges and blocking

fumble (**fuhm** buhl): dropping the ball

fund-raising (**fuhnd** rayz ing): collecting money for a specific cause

glamour (**glam** ur): fashion, charm, or appeal

Great Depression: the decade of the 1930s when many people in the United States had no jobs and were very poor

guaranteed: promised that something would happen

halfback: one of the backs stationed near the far left or right side

handoff: a play in which one player gives the ball to another

humble (**huhm** buhl): modest and not proud

imposing (im **poze** ing): impressive and grand

incorporated (in **kor** puh rate ed): made part of a legal business corporation

inducted (in **dukt** ed): to be added to an honored group

innovator (in uh **vay** tur): someone who takes a new and original approach

interception (in tur **sept** shuhn): in football, stealing another team's pass

law-abiding (**law** uh **bye** ding): obeying the laws of a government

letter: a fabric letter that can be sewn on a sweater to show that a player who plays on a high school team is important to the team

lopsided: unbalanced, with one side heavier, larger, or higher than the other

merge (**murj**): join together

motivator (**moh** tuh vay tur): someone who can make others feel enthusiastic and able to accomplish necessary tasks

nonprofit corporation: a business whose main purpose is something other than making money

opponent (uh **poh** nuhnt): someone who is against you in a fight, contest, debate, or election

profit (**prof** it): amount of money left after all of the costs of running a business have been subtracted from the money earned

publicity (puh **bliss** uh tee): information about a person or an event that is given out to get the public's attention or approval

punting (**puhnt** ing): kicking the ball to give it to the other team

reception (ri **sep** shuhn): response

referee: someone who supervises a sports game and makes sure the players follow the rules

reputation: a person's worth or character as judged by other people

resigned: gave up a job, a position, or an office voluntarily

rivalry (**rye** vuhl ree): an ongoing competition between 2 teams

roster: a list of people

scrimmage (**skrim** ij): in football, the rough contact that occurs as soon as the ball is picked up off the ground and snapped to another player

share: one of many equal parts into which a business is divided

shot put, discus, and broad jump: track competitions that involve throwing and jumping

signaled: sent a message or warning

slaughter (**slaw** tur): win by a wide margin

sophomore (sof mor): a student in the second year of high school or college

squad (skwahd): another name for a team

strategist (strat uh jist): someone who plans out how the team will play

strategy (strat uh jee): the plan a team uses to play the game

telegraphed (tel uh graft): sent a message in Morse code over a wire

thriving (thrive ing): doing well

tonsillitis (ton suh **ly** tiss): a throat infection

veteran (vet ur uhn): a player who has been a member of a team for many seasons

Reading Group Guide and Activities

Discussion Questions

- Like all of us, Curly Lambeau had both strengths and weaknesses. But since he was in a position of power, his personality made a large impact on those around him. Create one list of his strengths and one of his weaknesses. How did his strengths help his career? How did his weaknesses hurt it?

- Professional football has changed a great deal since the early years in which Curly Lambeau played and coached. In what ways has it changed? In what ways has it remained the same?

- Curly was certainly a sports hero in his own day. Think of sports heroes popular today. In what ways are they similar? In what ways are they different?

- Football was everything to Curly Lambeau. Discuss why you feel the game was so important to him. In what ways did his passion for it contribute to his success as a leader?

- Without Curly Lambeau, there would be no modern day Green Bay Packers. Can you think of another business that depended on one person for its existence? Can you think of another sports team? Compare and contrast the 2 experiences.

Activities

- Football was a much more dangerous sport when Curly Lambeau's career began. Use research from books and the Internet to create a time line that shows new safety regulations that protect players as much as possible.

- Think about the way football uniforms and equipment have changed over time, and create a flow chart with photos or drawings to show this process.

- Create a chart to show the Green Bay Packers' championship years and find out who the coaches and key players were for each championship season.

- The Green Bay Packers are the only community-owned professional football team. Contact the Green Bay Chamber of Commerce to ask about the impact the Green Bay Packers have had on the community of Green Bay. See if you can find out some of the businesses that make it possible for such a small city to support such a major team.

- Look up Curly's win/loss statistics as a coach. Compare them with statistics for 2 modern day coaches.

- Look at a play diagram. Make up your own play, using a similar system of marking.

To Learn More about Football and the Green Bay Packers

Anderson, Dave. *The Story of Football*. New York: HarperCollins Publishers, 1997.

Buckley, James. *America's Greatest Game: The Real Story of Football and the NFL*. New York: Hyperion, 1998.

Helmer, Diana Star. *The History of Football*. New York: PowerKids Press, 2000.

Nichols, John. *The Green Bay Packers*. Mankato, MN: Creative Education, 2001.

Nichols, John. *The History of the Green Bay Packers*. Mankato, MN: Creative Education, 2004.

Stewart, Mark. *The Green Bay Packers*. Chicago: Norwood House Press, 2007.

Acknowledgments

As a child, I remember driving past Lambeau Field on the way to family vacations in Michigan's Upper Peninsula. It was the era of Vince Lombardi and Bart Starr and Super Bowl victories, and, even though I was living in Chicago, I was a Packer fan. I am grateful to my father, my mother, and my grandmother for their love of the game, and the time we spent together watching the Packers in the glory days of the 1960s. This book allowed me to rediscover the Packers and something of their history.

I'm grateful to the Packers organization for their help. Sarah Quick, Tom Murphy, and Lee Remmel all provided valuable assistance. Art Daley, long-time sportswriter and Packer fan, was also very generous with his time.

The staff of the Wisconsin Historical Society Press have steered this book in its long march down the field toward the end zone. Bobbie Malone coached me tirelessly in getting the manuscript in shape. Erica Schock, John Nondorf, Elizabeth Boone, and Joel Heiman all provided help in design and production to complete the book's final drive.

I'm thankful to my sisters and my parents, to Simon and Celeste, and to Tom Pease, Barbara Chusid, and countless other friends for creating such good energy in my life. I am grateful to Charlie Knower, Cerisa, and Calli for reading the manuscript and giving me their suggestions and impressions, like good armchair quarterbacks should. Most of all, my wife, Heather, is a constant source of inspiration, support, and love. She's always there to encourage me to pick myself up and get back in for one more play. Plus, she's a huge Packer fan. To her, and to Packer fans everywhere, this book is dedicated.

Index

This index points you to the pages where you can read about persons, places, and ideas. If you do not find the word you are looking for, try to think of another word that means about the same thing.

Page numbers in **bold** means that there is a picture on that page.